WHO WE ARE

THE BLACK AMERICAN EXPERIENCE

Don Nardo

San Diego, CA

About the Author

Historian and award-winning author Don Nardo has written many books for young adults about American history and culture, among them *The Salem Witch Trials*; *The Sons of Liberty*; *The Declaration of Independence*; *The Mexican-American War*; biographies of presidents Thomas Jefferson, Andrew Johnson, and Franklin D. Roosevelt; and several volumes about Native American history and culture. Nardo lives with his wife, Christine, in Massachusetts.

© 2023 ReferencePoint Press, Inc.
Printed in the United States

For more information, contact:
ReferencePoint Press, Inc.
PO Box 27779
San Diego, CA 92198
www.ReferencePointPress.com

ALL RIGHTS RESERVED.
No part of this work covered by the copyright hereon may be reproduced or used in any form or by any means—graphic, electronic, or mechanical, including photocopying, recording, taping, web distribution, or information storage retrieval systems—without the written permission of the publisher.

LIBRARY OF CONGRESS CATALOGING-IN-PUBLICATION DATA

Names: Nardo, Don, 1947- author.
Title: The Black American experience / by Don Nardo.
Description: San Diego, CA : ReferencePoint Press, Inc., 2023. | Series: Who we are | Includes bibliographical references and index.
Identifiers: LCCN 2022034587 (print) | LCCN 2022034588 (ebook) | ISBN 9781678204686 (library binding) | ISBN 9781678204693 (ebook)
Subjects: LCSH: African Americans--History--Juvenile literature. | African Americans--Social conditions--Juvenile literature. | Slavery--United States--History--Juvenile literature. | United States--Race relations--History--Juvenile literature.
Classification: LCC E185 .N24 2023 (print) | LCC E185 (ebook) | DDC 305.896/073--dc23/eng/20220816
LC record available at https://lccn.loc.gov/2022034587
LC ebook record available at https://lccn.loc.gov/2022034588

CONTENTS

Black Americans: By the Numbers — 4

Introduction — 6
The Diversity of Black Americans

Chapter One — 9
Coming to America

Chapter Two — 18
Striving for Rights

Chapter Three — 27
Building Community

Chapter Four — 36
Embracing Identity

Chapter Five — 46
Facing Challenges

Source Notes — 55
For Further Research — 58
Index — 60
Picture Credits — 64

BLACK AMERICANS: BY THE NUMBERS

Total Population
- 41.1 million identify as Black American
- 46.9 million identify as Black American in combination with another ethnic group

Age Distribution

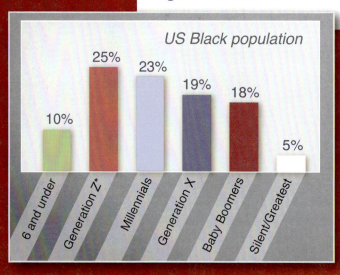

US Black population: 6 and under 10%, Generation Z* 25%, Millennials 23%, Generation X 19%, Baby Boomers 18%, Silent/Greatest 5%

* No chronological endpoint has been set for this group. For this analysis, Generation Z is defined by those who are ages seven to twenty-two in 2019.

Education
- High school diploma: 90.3%
- Bachelor's degree or higher: 28.1%

Life Expectancy
- Both men and women: 77.0 years
- Women: 79.8 years
- Men: 74.0 years

4

Five States with Largest Black American Populations

Median Household Income
- $44,000

Religion

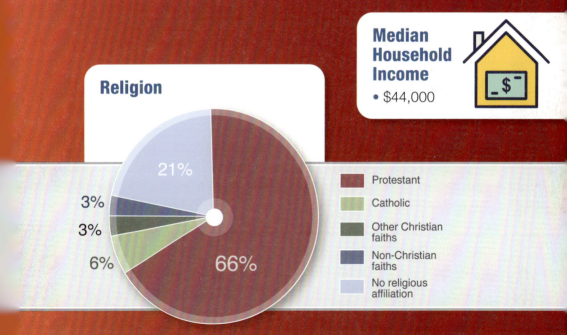

- 66% Protestant
- 6% Catholic
- 3% Other Christian faiths
- 3% Non-Christian faiths
- 21% No religious affiliation

Note: percentages do not add to 100 due to rounding.

INTRODUCTION

The Diversity of Black Americans

Black Americans do not fit neatly into one box. They live in rural communities and urban cityscapes. Politically speaking, many identify as Democrats, but others lean solidly Republican. Black Americans have held the highest political offices, including US president and secretary of state, and have sat on the nation's highest court, the Supreme Court. Black Americans have flown into space, created sublime melodies, and demonstrated feats of athletic prowess. They have worked as truck drivers, teachers, bookkeepers, engineers, farmers, doctors, and nurses. They have crafted riveting tales in books and for television and film. They worship in both Christian and non-Christian faiths. Many Black Americans are descended from slaves, but others came to the United States as immigrants.

Demographics expert Kiana Cox summarized these facts in a study of adult Black Americans she headed in 2021 for the Pew Research Center, a widely respected social polling organization. Like other Americans, she concluded that Black Americans "have diverse experiences and come from an array of backgrounds."[1] Indeed, the Black American community is not monolithic, or characterized mainly by the same views, opinions, and attitudes. Instead, says Alex Wade, a Black community organizer in Los Angeles, "the diversity and differences within [the Black community] are real. We come from different religious/spiritual beliefs and political practices. Believe it [or not], there are Black atheists and conservatives, but society would paint the picture that all Blacks are Christians and Democrats."[2]

Black Identity

As it turns out, however, one thing a majority of adult Black Americans do agree on is that being Black is very important to the way they see themselves as people. This was a key finding of the Pew Research Center study, which was published in 2022. Cox and her colleagues found that 76 percent, or slightly more than three-quarters, of those polled felt that way about being Black. That figure is extremely high, the researchers point out, when one considers that only 32 percent of adults in the general population—which includes Whites, Asians, Hispanics, and other non-Blacks—consider their race to be very important to their identity. Indeed, reemphasizing the huge proportion of Blacks who feel that way, Cox states:

> Whether Black people were born in the United States or outside of it, whether Black people identified as Black alone, Hispanic, or multiracial in addition to being Black, or whether they were younger or older . . . across all of those intersections, the idea that being Black was very or extremely important to how Black Americans view themselves, that was a very consistent finding for us.[3]

Black Americans are extremely diverse, but research shows that the majority do agree that being Black is very important to the way they see themselves.

Another point of agreement is that Black Americans have been subjected to racism and discrimination throughout much of US history. As a result, large numbers of Black Americans are extremely frustrated and at times fearful. These negative feelings came to a head in May 2020 when a Black Minneapolis man, George Floyd, was murdered by a police officer, an incident caught on video and broadcast around the world. In the days that followed, crowds of protesters (composed of people of all races) angrily demonstrated in hundreds of US cities and towns. A few weeks after Floyd's death, Jason Ellington, a Black marketing professional in Union, New Jersey, told an NPR interviewer how angry he was. "It is already hard enough that we have to fight within ourselves to become a better person," he said. "But there are countless forces working outside of ourselves that are also working against us and have been for generations."[4] Echoing those feelings, a Fort Lauderdale, Florida, Black man, Alexander Pittman, commented, "Being a Black man in America, you know you live by a different set of rules."[5]

Feeling Connected

Black Americans have found strength in their shared experiences as well as their diversity. This is true even when they come from different backgrounds and have different life experiences. Whether they were born here or immigrated from other nations; whether they are rich, poor, or middle-class; and whatever their religious beliefs "many Black Americans feel connected to each other,"[6] the Pew researchers state. This feeling of connection has been—and continues to be—an important part of the Black American experience.

CHAPTER ONE

Coming to America

Olaudah Equiano, the son of a chief of the West African Igbo tribe, was only eleven when one day in 1756 his entire life changed in a frightening instant. That day, he recalled more than thirty years later, "when all our people were gone out to their works as usual, and only I and my dear sister were left to mind the house, two men and a woman got over our walls, and in a moment seized us both. And, without giving us time to cry out, or make resistance, they stopped [gagged] our mouths, and ran off with us into the nearest wood."[7]

Having been snatched by members of a rival tribe, the two children were dragged from one African region to another until they reached the sea. There they were sold to European slave traders. Equiano later remembered:

> The first object which saluted my eyes when I arrived on the coast, was the sea, and a slave ship, which was then riding at anchor, and waiting for its cargo. These filled me with astonishment, which was soon converted into terror when I was carried on board. . . . [Soon I saw] a multitude of black people of every description chained together, every one of their countenances [faces] expressing dejection and sorrow.[8]

That ship took young Equiano, who became separated from his sister, on a nightmarish voyage across the ocean to the English colony of Virginia. There an English naval officer named Michael Henry Pascal bought him. In time Pascal took the youth to England and later to other lands. Pascal allowed Equiano to educate himself using the master's own books and in 1766 freed him. In the years that followed, Equiano became a well-known abolitionist in England. He published his autobiography in 1789, in part to educate White people about the horrors he had endured as a youngster.

Slave Life on Southern Plantations

Equiano's book is one of the most vivid surviving accounts of the horrendous Atlantic slave trade that operated from the late 1500s to the early 1800s. At first the Spanish and Portuguese and later the Dutch, French, and English, among others, bought or captured large numbers of Africans. They brought them to assorted colonies and plantations in the Americas, where the captured Africans labored in servitude.

By the mid-1700s a little over three hundred thousand Blacks lived in the thirteen English North American colonies, making up fully one-fifth of the population. Most were enslaved in Georgia, the Carolinas, and other southern states where they worked on cotton, rice, sugarcane, and tobacco plantations. The majority of the owners of those estates had fewer than fifty slaves each, though the biggest, wealthiest plantations each had a few hundred slaves.

In addition to picking cotton and other types of harvesting, most Black slaves typically did other hard, menial tasks, including ditchdigging, slaughtering livestock, and cutting down trees. In contrast, some slave owners saw the financial benefits of training a few of their male slaves to be blacksmiths, carpenters, and other skilled tradesmen. Some female slaves, meanwhile, cooked and did spinning, weaving, and sewing for the master's family.

Whatever their jobs on farms and plantations happened to be, the slaves did them because they had no choice. They were expected to follow orders given by their masters and the overseers those owners hired to manage the subjugated labor force. They were viewed as property. They had no rights or recourse. Slave owners had no interest in their wants or needs. Therefore, the late American historian Irwin Unger wrote, "the slaves' lives were not their own." They were not allowed to move from place to place

This picture depicts African slaves being taken on board a ship bound for the United States. Slaves had to endure brutal conditions on these voyages.

and could not express their feelings and opinions freely. Indeed, he adds, slavery denied them "those sacred rights of life, liberty, and the pursuit of happiness."[9]

This lack of basic human rights, rights that White Americans automatically enjoyed in that era, was based on the notion that the slaves were inferior beings. This arrogance and cruelty manifested itself in numerous other ways. On many plantations for instance, the food given to slaves was barely adequate to support the physical demands of their jobs. Also, most Black slaves lived in poorly insulated wooden shacks that were freezing in the winter. For most, clothing and bedding were equally inadequate.

Insufficient nutrition, unsanitary living conditions, and relentless hard work resulted in many illnesses. Malaria took a toll on the slaves who toiled on rice plantations, for example. Moreover, some masters forced their slaves to continue working even when they were ill or in serious pain. Not surprisingly, infant mortality—the incidence of death in infants—among Black slaves was alarmingly high, frequently surpassing 60 percent.

Cruelty, Fear, and Defiance

The physical rigors of slavery were often matched, or even exceeded, by emotional and psychological damage. Some of this stemmed from fear of threatened violence, which was at times carried out with horrendous cruelty. It was not uncommon for masters or overseers to brutalize slaves, sometimes for small or even nonexistent infractions. Among the typical punishments were whipping, shaving the head, and branding with hot irons. In 1771, when a Virginia planter placed a newspaper ad to help him locate his runaway slave, Peter, the text said in part, "I branded him S on the cheek, and R on the other. . . . I likewise had his hair cut off, which is long, when grown out."[10] Other, more severe penalties included amputating the ears or some of the toes of slaves, pulling out some of their teeth, slitting their noses, and scalding them with hot water.

Slaves also lived under the ever-present shadow of being sold to another master. Slave owners cared little about how their actions broke apart families. Sometimes they sold slaves because they wanted to make a financial profit. In other cases the sale was meant as a punishment. In addition, Unger pointed out, the threat of such separations could be a powerful form of discipline to keep slaves in line. Furthermore, he said, "slavery was at war with Black family life in other ways. Nowhere in the Old South did the law recognize the sanctity of slave marriages. To have done so would have limited the power of slaveholders to dispose of slaves as they wished."[11]

Nevertheless, many slaves were daring and enterprising in their defiance, more often than not in secret, of the master's rules. Male and female slaves often joined in marriages that they recognized as real, even if their owners did not. This was part of an array of

> "Nowhere in the Old South did the law recognize the sanctity of slave marriages. To have done so would have limited the power of slaveholders to dispose of slaves as they wished."[11]
>
> —Late American historian Irwin Unger

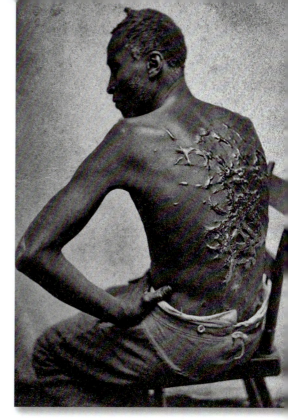

Masters or overseers frequently brutalized slaves, often for small or even nonexistent infractions. In this 1863 photo, a man shows scars from a whipping that he received as a slave in Mississippi.

cultural customs they observed inside their ramshackle quarters, where the Whites who controlled them were unable to see or hear them. Through cultivating such underground cultures, many slaves managed to hold on to their innate senses of humanity, decency, and hope for a better future. It was common to gather in the evenings to tell stories about the family's ancestors in Africa or elsewhere. Parents also taught their children useful skills they had acquired over time, such as hunting, fishing, the healing arts, and more.

Not All Blacks Were Enslaved

Not all Black people in the American colonies, and in the new country that formed in 1776, were slaves. In the late 1850s, African American historian Henry Louis Gates Jr. notes, "there were a total of 488,070 free Blacks living in the United States, about 10 percent of the entire Black population."[12] Roughly half of those free Blacks lived in the North, he says, and the other half in the South. Most of them dwelled in cities, where they found work as laborers or tradespeople, although a minority farmed small plots in the countryside.

Free Blacks obtained that status in various ways. In some cases, the slave owner freed his slaves at the time of his death. A well-known example was Virginia planter and politician John Randolph. Before his passing in 1833, he made a will that stated in

The Inhumane Middle Passage

Several eyewitness descriptions of the Atlantic slave trade's Middle Passage—that is, the voyage across the Atlantic Ocean from Africa to the Americas—have survived. They paint a picture of incredibly cruel and inhumane conditions aboard the slave ships. One of those accounts appeared in the 1789 autobiography of the English abolitionist Olaudah Equiano, who himself had endured that hellish journey in the late 1750s. He recalled that when he was first taken belowdecks, the smell of sweat, urine, and vomit combined was nauseating. "I received such an [odor] in my nostrils as I had never experienced in my life," he wrote. "So that with the loathsomeness of the stench and crying together, I became so sick and low that I was not able to eat."

In 1788 another witness, English doctor Alexander Falconbridge, penned an account that described how in the ship's hold the slaves had to lie on their backs, their bodies crammed into spaces measuring only 18 inches (46 cm) high. Therefore, they could barely change position. Also, he said, the slaves were chained by the neck and legs. "The sense of misery and suffocation is so great that [they are often] driven to frenzy," he reported.

Quoted in *Africans in America*, "Equiano's Autobiography," PBS. www.pbs.org.

Quoted in Howard Zinn, *A People's History of the United States*. New York: HarperCollins, 2005, p. 28.

---

part, "I give and bequeath to all my slaves their freedom, heartily regretting that I have ever been the owner of one."[13] When he died, his brother contested the will, and thirteen years passed before a Virginia court upheld Randolph's wishes. Using $8,000 Randolph had allotted in the will for resettlement costs, his former slaves—numbering close to four hundred—made new homes in Ohio.

Black Immigration: From Rare to Common

By the time of the Civil War, the nation's Black population numbered close to 5 million. That number began to grow in the twentieth century, with immigration from Africa and the Caribbean. The vast majority of these immigrants traveled to the United States from regions where poverty was common and occupational opportunities limited. Typically, they immigrated to America with high hopes of finding good jobs, achieving success, and building secure futures for their families.

For the most part, these immigrants came from Nigeria, Ethiopia, and Ghana in Africa or from one of the Caribbean islands. Large numbers of Caribbean immigrants came to the United States between the late 1800s and 1930 and again between 1941 and 1950. A third wave of Black immigrants, this time from Africa and the Caribbean, occurred between 1980 and 2019.

A Shared Struggle

Most of these immigrants in this third wave settled in New York, Texas, Florida, California, and Massachusetts. Most commonly they gravitated toward big cities, especially New York City, Dallas, Los Angeles, Miami, and Boston. This choice was based on the belief that finding jobs and housing and establishing credit would be easier for them in urban areas than in rural ones. Also, big cities were most often where some of them had family or friends from earlier waves of immigrants, people who could help the newcomers get settled.

The vast majority of Black immigrants who arrived between 1980 and 2019 did find work. Of the males, those who were well educated became businessmen, scientists, and artists, while the rest ended up in service occupations such as store clerk, cook, waiter, or taxi driver. Similarly, the more educated women in the third wave became teachers, nurses, and office workers, while others worked mainly in service jobs.

Like all immigrants to America, those from Africa and the Caribbean faced not only finding work and places to live but also fitting into and feeling comfortable within the existing society. For the Black immigrants in particular, this was sometimes hard because in their home countries most of the population was Black. Because this was the norm, being Black was not an identity that had to be nurtured. "When I came to America, I found myself taking on a new identity," says novelist Chimamanda Ngozi Adichie, who came to America from Nigeria in 1996. "Rather, I found a new identity thrust upon me. I became black in America. And I really hadn't thought of myself as black in Nigeria."[14] There, she explains, people identify instead with their religious or ethnic group.

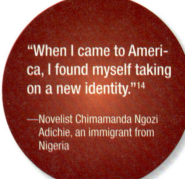

"When I came to America, I found myself taking on a new identity."[14]

—Novelist Chimamanda Ngozi Adichie, an immigrant from Nigeria

Singer Nabil Amadu, who immigrated to Los Angeles from Ghana in 2012, agrees. "We don't have that idea of blackness," back in Africa, he remarks. Rather, he says, "we identify with a tribe. I'm forced to think that maybe because of my upbringing from a foreign place, maybe I don't see the same things that African-Americans see."[15]

However, no matter where they were born and how they view themselves and life in general, native-born Black Americans and

Civil rights marchers are pictured in 2013 in Washington, DC. Black Americans have struggled for generations to achieve freedom and civil rights.

The Need for Printed Narratives by Black Immigrants

Ewaoluwa Ogundana, who turned twenty-two in 2022, came to the United States from Nigeria with her parents when she was four. The family settled in Maryland, and Ewa, as she is known to family and friends, received an excellent education in US schools, including Trinity Washington University. Although she feels like she is on her way to achieving the proverbial American dream, she also notes that it can be difficult for immigrants from Africa to relate to American culture. In part, she says, this is because there are few existing books by such immigrants that tell about the struggles they have endured. "The first time I read a book written by a Black immigrant author was not until my first semester of college," she points out.

> Reading that book made me feel seen, celebrated, and helped me to know that there are people like me who share similar stories, and who are and can be notable authors. I wish that I didn't have to wait until college to read a book that reflected my background, and I can only imagine how much more enriching my K–12 experience would have been if Black immigrant narratives were more celebrated and included in the curriculum.

Ewaoluwa Ogundana, "The Importance of Including Black Immigrant Narratives in K–12 Education," New America, April 4, 2022. www.newamerica.org.

Black immigrants do share the sense of long-term struggle. Black Americans whose ancestors arrived on slave ships struggled for generations to achieve freedom and civil rights. Similarly, Black immigrants struggled with problems in their home nations that led them to seek better lives in America. Amadu, for one, recognizes that shared background and sees that all Black Americans ultimately seek the same fundamental things—respect and equal opportunity. Perhaps, he says, "we can understand that we share a common struggle."[16]

CHAPTER TWO

Striving for Rights

On New Year's Day in 1834, a young Black slave named William, who was about twenty years old at the time, was in Louisville, Kentucky. He had been taken there by boat by his master, a well-to-do Missouri farmer and merchant on a routine business trip. During the daylight hours, William slipped away from the docks and hid in some nearby woods until nightfall and then quietly made his way northward on foot. His intent was to reach a state where Black people were free, and he soon found himself in Ohio, which had outlawed slavery in 1802.

On his first day in that state, by chance William encountered an elderly man named Wells Brown, who immediately put him at ease. A Quaker who vehemently opposed slavery, Brown offered to aid the youth in whatever ways he could. After about two weeks, William decided to continue northward. Just before he left, Brown offered to give the youth his own name. As a result, thereafter the former slave went by the name William Wells Brown.

Proud of his new name, the young man at first settled in Buffalo, New York, where he worked for a while for a steamboat service. Over time he learned to read, educated himself, and became determined to help other Black Americans escape the ordeals of slavery. He strongly felt that that horrid institution brought shame to the country by contradicting its high ideals. "While the people of the United States boast of their freedom," he later wrote, "they at the same time keep three millions of their own citizens in chains."[17]

In the early 1840s Brown joined the ranks of the abolitionists. People of all races and walks of life, they strove to abolish slavery. Brown's speeches and writings condemning that institution eventually became widely known throughout the United States and Britain.

The Abolitionists

As the number of abolitionists grew, the cause began scoring victories. In the infant United States, for example, all the states north of Maryland abolished slavery between 1777 and 1804. Also, in March 1807 Britain banned the Atlantic slave trade, and US lawmakers followed suit a few months later.

Those actions did not bring an end to slavery, however. The fight to eliminate the institution of slavery in the United States fell to the nation's abolitionists. In addition to numerous Whites in their number, most notably newspaper editor William Lloyd Garrison, hundreds of Black abolitionists joined the movement. Some of the latter had, like William Wells Brown, begun as slaves and later gained their freedom. Probably the most famous member of that group was Frederick Douglass. After escaping slavery in Maryland in 1838 at age twenty, he became a tireless writer, orator, and lecturer who eventually conferred with and influenced President Abraham Lincoln.

In the first of Douglass's three autobiographies, *Narrative of the Life of Frederick Douglass, an American Slave*, published in 1845, he described the lives of Southern slaves, often in graphic detail. This powerful work became essential reading for all abolitionists. Douglass did not mince words, including when he sometimes criticized White Northerners who disliked the idea of slavery but largely ignored and remained silent about the everyday ugly realities of that practice. "I have often been utterly astonished, since I came to the North," he said in the first autobiography, "to find persons who could speak of the singing, among slaves, as evidence of their contentment and happiness. It is impossible to conceive of a greater mistake. Slaves sing most when they are most unhappy. The songs of the slave represent the sorrows of his heart; and he is relieved by them, only as an aching heart is relieved by its tears."[18]

"Slaves sing most when they are most unhappy. The songs of the slave represent the sorrows of his heart; and he is relieved by them, only as an aching heart is relieved by its tears."[18]

—Black abolitionist and writer Frederick Douglass

Douglass was no less critical of the US government for its failure to abolish slavery. "There is not a nation on earth guilty of practices more shocking and bloody than are the people of these United States at this very hour,"[19] he wrote in 1852. This frankness, which other abolitionists saw as refreshing, was typical of his editorials in the abolitionist newspaper he established in 1847—the *North Star*.

Among the other former slaves who became prominent abolitionists was Henry H. Garnet. In 1843 he gained national attention for calling on slaves to rebel against their masters. Better known today, however, is Harriet Tubman, who fled her Maryland master in 1849 at age twenty-seven and thereafter became a key figure in the Underground Railroad. Abolitionists employed that secret system of safe houses to smuggle Southern slaves northward. In thirteen daring missions, staged in the darkness of night, this fearless woman led some seventy slaves to freedom, among them the members of her own family. (For these fantastic feats she earned the affectionate nickname of Moses, after the famous biblical prophet said to have led the enslaved Hebrews out of Egypt.)

Black Americans who had been born free also played important roles in the abolitionist movement. Mary Ann Shadd Cary, for

This nineteenth-century photo shows former slave and Underground Railroad conductor Harriet Tubman (left), her stepdaughter (second from left), and husband (third from left). With them are extended family members, and former slaves that Tubman helped during the Civil War.

instance, allowed her home to be part of the Underground Railroad. Meanwhile, David Walker became widely known for his 1829 pamphlet titled *Appeal to the Coloured Citizens of the World*, which forcefully denounced the brutality of slavery. With the aid of some church leaders, he was able to smuggle thousands of copies of that provocative document onto plantations across the American South.

The Jim Crow Era

Eventually, demands for abolition by an ever-growing faction of Northerners and the entrenched economic and social forces supporting slavery in the South collided hard enough to ignite the American Civil War. That conflict, fought from 1861 to 1865, had a number of diverse causes. But chief among them was the issue of slavery, including whether it should be allowed to expand into new states as they entered the Union.

Soon after the North won the war, Black slaves officially gained their freedom through the Thirteenth Amendment to the Constitution, ratified in December 1865. The Fourteenth Amendment, ratified in July 1868, granted the former slaves citizenship and equal protection under the law. These landmark new laws represented an important step forward for African American civil rights. But they did not suddenly bring Blacks the respect and fair treatment that Whites enjoyed simply by virtue of their skin color. Deep-seated and overt racism lingered after the war, especially in the South.

Inspired by anti-Black hatred and a twisted belief in their own superiority, in the late 1870s White Southern leaders began passing so-called Jim Crow laws. These kept many Blacks from registering to vote or from actually voting. They also kept Black people from running for office or serving on juries, as well as segregated Blacks from Whites in schools, housing, restaurants, and public restrooms. Moreover, the Black versions of these facilities were nearly always substandard in quality.

African Americans who broke Jim Crow laws were intimidated, beaten, and sometimes outright killed, frequently by lynching. The Equal Justice Initiative (EJI), headquartered in Montgomery,

Alabama, estimates that more than forty-four hundred Blacks were lynched, mostly in Southern states, from 1877 to 1950. This, an EJI spokesperson states, "was terrorism, a widely supported phenomenon used to enforce racial subordination and segregation. Lynchings were violent and public events that traumatized Black people throughout the country and were largely tolerated by state and federal officials."[20]

"O God, is there no redress, no peace, no justice in this land for us?"[21]

—Black educator Ida B. Wells

Thus, during the Jim Crow era, progress in Blacks' quest for equal rights largely stagnated in much of the United States. In 1883 African American educator Ida B. Wells summed up the frustration of the vast majority of Blacks, writing, "O God, is there no redress, no peace, no justice in this land for us?"[21]

Challenging Segregation

It certainly appeared to Wells and many other Black Americans of that era that they and their descendants might never enjoy the fruits of justice in the United States. Yet some leaders within local Black communities in various cities did their best to fight and, they hoped, even reverse some of those unfair statutes. One of the most courageous and well-known efforts of that sort occurred in New Orleans, Louisiana, between 1880 and the mid-1890s. There, in 1879 local White officials passed laws strictly segregating schools, forcing Black students to attend classes in separate buildings from White students.

Banding together, a group of prominent Black citizens became activists who tried repeatedly to stop this segregation of the races. Initially, they held demonstrations in the street, and when that had no effect they filed lawsuits. Next, according to the museum and research center known as the Historic New Orleans Collection, they started a Black social club dedicated to ensuring that "our rights as citizens of this State and of the United States [are] protected and respected."[22] In 1889 the club members started a newspaper, the *Crusader*, in which they printed editorials demanding that White leaders respect Black rights.

When none of these efforts succeeded, the Black activists sought redress from the US Supreme Court. They singled out a new law passed in 1890 by the state of Louisiana. It barred "colored people" from sitting in the White seating sections of trains. Blacks were already segregated from these sections. At the time, the term *colored* often referred to mixed-race persons, many of whom could pass for White. The activists realized that one of their number, Homer Plessy, was one-eighth Black and looked White. He seemed to be the perfect person to test the 1890 law. In June 1892 Plessy purchased a train ticket and boarded a passenger car. Then he told the conductor that he was a colored person and sat down in the car's White section. When told to move, Plessy refused and, as expected, was arrested.

As the activists had hoped, the case went all the way to the Supreme Court, where it became known as *Plessy v. Ferguson*. The plaintiffs' basic argument was that it was frequently quite hard to tell who was Black or White. Therefore, the law in question was unreasonable. The high court did not accept this claim, however.

Blacks Who Fought in Union Forces

One way that Black Americans fought for their rights during the Civil War was by fighting in the Union armed forces. Most of the Blacks who joined up did so beginning in early 1863, when the Union began an official effort to enroll them. In all, approximately 186,000 Black soldiers served in the Union army and almost 30,000 fought in the navy. Indeed, in the war's last two years, close to 10 percent of the total Union fighting forces were Black, more than half of them former slaves. The Black soldiers and sailors served with distinction. A little more than a third of them gave their lives in the effort, and twenty-four received the Congressional Medal of Honor for extraordinary courage on the battlefield.

Perhaps the most famous Black military unit in the conflict was the Fifty-Fourth Massachusetts Regiment, commanded by a White officer in his twenties—Robert Gould Shaw. He led his men in the renowned charge on a Confederate stronghold, Fort Wagner, in South Carolina in July 1863. The brave but unsuccessful attack, in which Shaw and 40 percent of the Black soldiers died, was accurately and graphically depicted in the highly acclaimed 1989 film *Glory*.

In 1896 it ruled in favor of the state, asserting that the law was perfectly constitutional. This ruling became a crucial justification for state-sanctioned segregation and discrimination throughout the South for decades to come.

Positive Social and Legal Changes

Fortunately for Black Americans, and the country as a whole, over time the narrow-minded prejudices that had made the perverse *Plessy* decision possible steadily gave way to more progressive and just societal views. After the end of World War II in 1945, increasing numbers of Americans became more tolerant than in the past. Many pointed out that thousands of African Americans had fought and even died for the country in the conflict. Yet when they returned home, the Black veterans were denied several basic civil rights. More and more Americans of all walks of life came to see this as unjust.

A number of positive social and legal changes followed. Some were initiated by presidential order and the courts. For instance, in 1948 President Harry Truman integrated Blacks and Whites in the armed forces. (Before that, Blacks had fought in separate units from Whites.) And in 1954 in the *Brown v. Board of Education* case, the Supreme Court struck down *Plessy v. Ferguson* and ruled that racially segregated schools were unjust.

In the years that followed, ordinary citizens entered the fray as well. In 1960 four Black North Carolina college students sat down at the lunch counter of a department store in Greensboro. Protesting that Blacks were not allowed to eat in White-owned stores, they sat quietly for hours, even though no one served them. Similar nonviolent demonstrations took place in over one hundred US cities in the weeks and months that followed. Eventually, some store owners gave in, seeing that integrating their lunch counters was the decent thing to do.

During this same period, groups of so-called Freedom Riders, often young Black and White people, challenged restrictions on non-Whites using buses, trains, and airplanes in Southern

The Freedom Riders Encounter Violence

The well-known 1961 civil rights activists known as Freedom Riders were initially motivated by the attempt to test a 1960 Supreme Court decision, *Boynton v. Virginia*, which declared that segregation of interstate transportation facilities, among them bus terminals, was unconstitutional. Seeing that nearly all Southern towns and cities ignored the ruling, Black and White volunteers traveled into the South on buses and trains and tried to use Whites-only waiting rooms and restrooms.

The first known violent reaction to their protests occurred on May 12, 1961, in Rock Hill, South Carolina. A Black seminary student named John Lewis and two other Freedom riders were brutally assaulted as they tried to enter a Whites-only waiting area. Though injured, the three survived, and later, in the 1980s, Lewis became an influential US congressman. Photos of that and subsequent vicious attacks on Freedom Riders appeared on newspaper front pages across the country and around the world, drawing widespread attention to the activists' cause. Such publicity helped make these protests ultimately successful. In response to the riders' efforts, in late 1961 the federal government issued rules banning segregation in interstate transit terminals.

states. They repeatedly rode through those states, despite being frequently arrested and sometimes attacked and beaten by angry White mobs.

These and other civil rights protests culminated in the historic 1963 march on Washington, DC. There, Black minister and civil rights activist Martin Luther King Jr. gave the memorable keynote speech. "I have a dream," he told the crowd of more than a quarter-million people, "that my four little children will one day live in a nation where they will not be judged by the color of their skin but by the content of their character."[23]

Even more historic were the events of the following two years. Spearheaded by a progressive president, Lyndon Johnson, the Civil Rights Act of 1964 prohibited both segregation in public places and discrimination in employment based on race, religion, or national origin. The Voting Rights Act of 1965 eliminated legal barriers at the state and local levels that had prevented many Black Americans from voting.

Famous civil rights activist Dr. Martin Luther King Jr. makes his "I Have a Dream" speech during the March on Washington, DC, in 1963.

Hope for a Better Future

The landmark civil rights protests, court cases, and legislation of the 1950s and 1960s improved the social and economic position of many Black Americans. Nevertheless, most Blacks, and many Whites too, recognized that some deep-seated biases against Black people still lingered. Discrimination against Blacks continued in various sectors of the country in the succeeding decades. Hope that such inequities would be eliminated over time was captured in the song "We Shall Overcome," which had become the anthem of the civil rights movement. Bolstering that hope for a better future, Johnson sent a powerful message to all Americans. When demanding that Congress pass the 1965 Voting Rights Act, he ended the speech with the words, "And we *shall* overcome."[24]

CHAPTER THREE

Building Community

In the wake of the Civil War and the end of slavery in 1865, Black people in both the North and South faced the prospect of building new, hopefully successful and prosperous lives and futures for their families. Many of their number hoped that their social positions in American society would significantly improve. Perhaps they might even have a shot at obtaining the benefits of what a later American historian would call "the American dream." It was a society "in which each man and each woman shall be able to attain to the fullest stature of which they are innately capable, and be recognized by others for what they are, regardless of the fortuitous circumstances of birth or position."[25]

To the average Black American in the post–Civil War era, the idea of having that sort of fair and happy life and choosing where to achieve it was inspiring and exciting. But it was also daunting. For decades most Black Americans had been blocked from choosing where they could live, starting a business, owning property, and so forth. Initially, it was slavery that had kept many Blacks from doing those things. Later, a combination of Jim Crow laws in the South and anti-Black bias and discrimination in banking and housing in White communities nationwide did the same.

One way to get around such bias, some prominent Blacks proposed, was for Blacks to band together and build their own viable, prosperous communities. These, they pointed out, would be reasonably safe spaces where Black family life, culture, education, and wealth creation would finally have a chance to flourish. In the first five decades following the Civil War, several of these Black enclaves arose. As Black historian Shennette Garrett-Scott puts it, in fashioning the Black enclaves, "African Americans were living out their vision of the American dream under the kinds of really difficult circumstances that racism left them with, but they were still thriving, and they were creating culture and they were creating opportunity and hope and progress for their communities."[26]

The Harlem of the South

Of these large Black communities, one of the first and most successful was the Jackson Ward district of Richmond, Virginia. Several prominent Black entrepreneurs, or enterprising businesspeople, contributed to its founding and growth. Chief among them was Maggie L. Walker. Born in 1864 in Richmond, she received an excellent education thanks to money from a rich White woman who had employed her mother as a cook. As a young adult, Walker proved herself to be an energetic and brilliant businesswoman who started several shops and other commercial ventures, all of them successful. At age thirty-eight, for instance, she opened a local newspaper, the *St. Luke Herald*. A few other Black entrepreneurs followed her lead, and the Jackson Ward area started to bloom economically.

A Renaissance in New York

Lying roughly in the center of New York City's Manhattan borough, Harlem has been a potent model for Black American economic and social achievement for over a century. Originally a haven for Dutch settlers in the 1660s, in the following two and a half centuries, Italian, German, Irish, and Jewish settlers occupied the area. The infusion of large numbers of Black Americans into Harlem began in the first decade of the twentieth century, and in the years that followed, many Blacks settled there. Some were accomplished in a wide range of trades, while others were merchants, educators, scholars, writers, painters, and musicians. This wide range of talents and abilities economically and culturally supercharged the community, and the 1920s witnessed an outburst of financial success and artistic achievement that collectively came to be known as the Harlem Renaissance. A few of the hundreds of famous Harlem residents of that period included writers Langston Hughes and Zora Neale Hurston, singers Josephine Baker and Billie Holiday, Shakespearean actor Paul Robeson, musicians Louis Armstrong and Duke Ellington, and journalist and publisher Marcus Garvey.

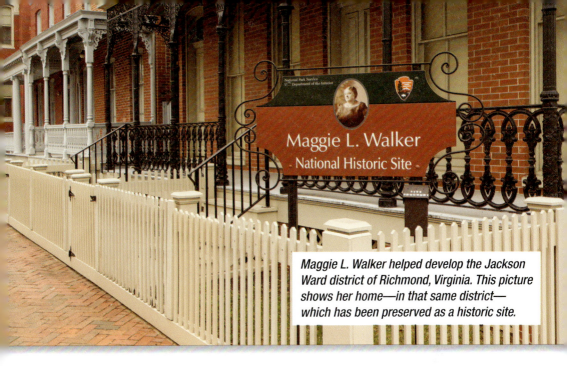

Maggie L. Walker helped develop the Jackson Ward district of Richmond, Virginia. This picture shows her home—in that same district—which has been preserved as a historic site.

Not long after starting the *Herald*, Walker made the single most crucial step in expanding that Black enclave. Like other Black leaders there and across the nation, she realized that the main obstacle to people, including Blacks, who sought to start a new business was finding sufficient start-up money. The problem was that most White banks would not lend money to Blacks, or if they did, they charged high interest rates that few Black people could afford to pay.

Walker saw that the solution was to create a Black-owned bank. "Let us put our moneys together," she told a group of prominent local Blacks in 1901. "Let us use our moneys; let us put our money . . . [toward loans that will be made] among ourselves, and reap the benefit ourselves. Let us have a bank that will take the nickels and turn them into dollars."[27] Walker subsequently became the first Black American woman to own a bank—the St. Luke Penny Savings. It opened its doors for business on November 2, 1903. On the first day alone, 280 people deposited money totaling roughly $8,000 (equivalent to almost $270,000 today).

Thanks in large measure to Walker's vision and tireless efforts, Jackson Ward blossomed. In the years that followed, thousands of Black Americans of all walks of life flocked there hoping to build better lives for themselves. And Richmond's Black enclave acquired the nickname of the "Harlem of the South," in reference to the successful Black community that arose in New York City in the same period.

Greenwood: From Success to Ashes

The same sort of entrepreneurial spirit that had made Jackson Ward a Black American success story in the early twentieth century was repeated in several other American cities in that same period. In addition to Harlem, among the best known and productive were Washington, DC's U-Street and Birmingham, Alabama's Fourth Avenue District. In reaction to widespread racism in that period, writes Black journalist Brianna Rhodes, "Black neighborhoods provided a sense of belonging, serving as a space not only to garner wealth, but also to celebrate Black culture."[28]

Although all of these, along with other similar Black districts, were successful to one degree or another, most historians think that one particularly stood out. It was the Greenwood sector of Tulsa, Oklahoma. Despite the fact that most Black urban communities bore the nickname "Black Wall Street," the one in Tulsa was widely viewed as *the* Black Wall Street because for a short time span it appears to have been the most economically successful.

Greenwood's path to that success began in 1905, when a small group of Black businesspeople bought a strip of land in Tulsa. In rapid succession, two local newspapers opened there, followed by grocery stores; a high school; variety stores; doctors', dentists', and lawyers' offices; a hospital; ballparks; and picnic grounds. Also, a Black businessman erected the Stradford Hotel. With fifty-four luxury suites, it was the biggest Black-owned hotel in the country. Altogether, by 1920 the Greenwood area boasted some two thousand homes and thriving businesses.

"Black neighborhoods provided a sense of belonging, serving as a space not only to garner wealth, but also to celebrate Black culture."[28]

—Journalist Brianna Rhodes

A New Black Wall Street in Georgia

One day in 2018, Lecester Allen, a Black Georgia philanthropist, watched a TV program about the 1921 destruction of Greenwood, the Black Wall Street in Tulsa, Oklahoma. Inspired to create a Black shopping district based in part on Greenwood, Allen initially used the resources of his own company, Allen Entrepreneurial Institute. With help from an investment expert, in November 2021 Allen opened the New Black Wall Street Market in Stonecrest, Georgia. According to writer, editor, and reporter Ronda Racha Penrice:

> The market, just over 15 miles east of Atlanta, feels different. The space's layout and decor imitates a downtown shopping district. Professional greeters say hello to patrons as they walk in. The website lists 45 shops open for business at the market, including an African textile museum, shoe boutiques, local jewelers, an art gallery, bookstore, and tax services, all designed with Black consumers in mind.

Ronda Racha Penrice, "We Took a Walk Down the New Black Wall Street. Here's What We Learned," Capital B Atlanta, February 8, 2022. https://atlanta.capitalbnews.org.

The problem was that in general, high levels of economic success in the country's Black enclaves frequently raised the ire of many neighboring Whites. Some of the latter felt that if African Americans made such large gains, it must be at the expense of Whites. It did not help that during Greenwood's boom years Tulsa had become the hometown of several members of the racist terrorist organization known as the Ku Klux Klan, which deeply resented the success of local Blacks. In the words of historian Paul Gardullo, "By 1921, Tulsa had developed into a powder keg of racial resentment waiting for a spark to ignite [it]."[29]

That horrifying ignition occurred on June 1, 1921, as hundreds of Whites, some armed with machine guns, swept into Greenwood. As the rioters shot people in the streets and torched buildings, several airplanes from a nearby airfield repeatedly swooped in and dropped firebombs. Almost every structure in a thirty-five-block area burned, and the White rioters threatened to kill any Tulsa firefighters who tried to put out the flames. When

This picture shows the Greenwood section of Tulsa, Oklahoma, after the 1921 riots that left almost every structure in a thirty-five-block area destroyed and nearly three hundred Black people dead.

the massacre ended, close to three hundred Black people lay dead. At least eight hundred more had been wounded, and many thousands of others were left homeless.

Greenwood's Rebirth

It remains a testament to the courage and resilience of Greenwood's survivors that in a few years' time they rebuilt parts of the ravaged community. That initial attempt at revitalization was not destined to last, however. In the 1960s a major freeway was constructed in the area's midst, and many homes and businesses disappeared to make way for big stretches of pavement.

And yet the passage of time has demonstrated that the powerful spirit of the Greenwood community has not been eradicated. From the early 2000s on, its economy began to rebound a second time. In the words of journalist Amber Gibson, "Today, Greenwood is rising again. A spate of new businesses ranging from workout studios to art galleries have created a renaissance of sorts in the Greenwood district. . . . There's so much optimism in Greenwood now, but it was a long hard road to make these streets feel like a safe haven and celebration of Black success once more."[30]

"Today, Greenwood is rising again."[30]

—Journalist Amber Gibson

Gibson's words "Greenwood is rising again" are especially apt because among the large-scale projects spearheading the enclave's ongoing rebirth is Greenwood Rising, a magnificent new museum. Funded by a special centennial committee that formed in 2015 with members from several of Tulsa's civic groups, the structure opened in 2021 and has attracted thousands of visitors from around the globe.

More than forty new Black-owned businesses had grown up in the museum's vicinity in the decade or so before it opened. Over thirty of those owners are women, who together pump over $5 million annually into Tulsa's economy. One of their number, Venita Cooper, who runs the colorful footwear shop Silhouette Sneakers & Art, says she owes a debt to the local owners who came before her. "I continue to be inspired," she says, "by the Black entrepreneurs who paved the way for me and [I] wanted to carry on their legacy in the same place."[31] Like all the Black businesspeople in the district, she is excited about the future, pointing out that several more Black-owned enterprises are slated to open in the mid-2020s.

Communal Cooperation in New Orleans

Cooper has not been alone in drawing inspiration from the refusal of the Greenwood community to disappear into history's proverbial dustbin. Over the years, the Greenwood story has either set an example for or been matched by similar outbursts of Black entrepreneurship. These have occurred not only in the United States but also beyond its borders.

Among these efforts is one ongoing in New Orleans. There local Black leaders and business owners are working with the American Friends Service Committee (AFSC). Originally a Quaker group that promoted world peace, over time it expanded its humanitarian efforts to include building productive, prosperous urban communities. Dee Dee Green, a Black program director for the organization, says that the AFSC "has worked to positively influence and mobilize communities of color . . . through education, organizing, and economics to realize sustainable and equitable Black communities.

We are working toward a future where Black communities are self-determined; realize their capacity to create change; and take actions that lead to social and cultural transformation."[32]

One way that the AFSC has been working to effect that transformation is by increasing fresh food supplies in New Orleans' predominantly Black neighborhoods. Much of the food comes from local gardens created and maintained by community members. The resulting food not only supplies local stores but is also sometimes shared among individual residents. In its initial year of operation alone, the project distributed around 5,100 pounds (2,313 kg) of produce to roughly 790 local families. "It's our neighborhood," states one of those residents. "It's an opportunity to uplift our people by feeding each other physically and communally. These events are an expression of values like caring for each other and belonging to something bigger than ourselves. Sharing food connects us to each other, the Black growers and farmers, and the land that is vital to our survival."[33]

Seattle and Beyond

Meanwhile, about 2,700 miles (4,345 km) northwest of New Orleans, a section of Seattle, Washington, is undergoing a similar type of expanding prosperity. Africatown Community Land Trust (ACLT), a Seattle-based organization, is buying and developing land on which to expand the local Black community. The strategy is to use such land for the benefit of local Black businesspeople and homeowners. Thanks to these efforts, in 2022 that enclave broke ground for Africatown Plaza, a $60 million project featuring 126 units of affordable housing, plus extensive studios for local Black artisans and shop owners.

ACLT's directors see their community's ongoing expansion as beneficial for Seattle's overall economy. They also view it as a test case for other Black economic and cultural enclaves across the nation. ACLT's president, K.W. Garrett, continues to oversee a series of lectures with compelling titles such as "Building New Black Wall Streets." These have been attended by representa-

K.W. Garrett is president of the Africatown Community Land Trust, a Seattle-based organization that is buying and developing land on which to expand the local Black community. He is pictured here speaking at a Juneteenth Freedom March in 2020.

tives of Black communities as far afield as Boston, Pittsburgh, the US Virgin Islands, and Nova Scotia, Canada. To them, Garrett explains and defends his decision to call such Black districts "Africatowns," saying, "When we think about any community of Chinese, you know, outside of China, you know what it's called? It's called Chinatown. And then when we think about our communities of people of African descent, Black people, here in America and other places, what are those communities called?"[34]

Thus, just as Greenwood's ongoing revival inspired several other Black neighborhoods to find ways to revitalize, in turn those efforts are inspiring still others across North America. Many diverse social and economic factors have helped stimulate a "resurgence of support for Black businesses," Brianna Rhodes points out. "And today Black Americans are using these neighborhoods as a blueprint to create their own enclaves and ensure their ancestors' legacy and history continues to live on."[35]

CHAPTER FOUR

Embracing Identity

In 1737, thirty-nine years before the British American colonies broke free of Britain and established the United States, a child was born to a slave woman on a plantation in Charleston, South Carolina. The infant's first name was Andrew. And because it was customary for slaves to take the last names of their masters, he became Andrew Bryan, after his master, Jonathan Bryan.

Unlike most other American slave owners of that era, Jonathan Bryan believed it was his duty to bring his slaves into the Christian faith. Preaching to slaves was then frowned upon by most Whites in the Southern colonies. And at one point, after Bryan moved to Georgia, the colony's leaders reprimanded him and forbade him to preach to slaves belonging to other owners.

Bryan obeyed that directive but continued to preach to his own slaves, including young Andrew. In time, Andrew began preaching to other slaves himself. With his master's permission, the young man erected a modest shack that over time expanded into a church that became widely popular among local Blacks. Initially, a number of Georgian planters feared that the members of Andrew's congregation might influence their own slaves. They brutally whipped Andrew and threw him in jail. Fortunately for Andrew, Bryan rushed to his defense and got him released.

Eventually, most of Georgia's leaders came around to the opinion that slaves *should* be converted to Christianity. And in 1788 Andrew Bryan, now in his fifties, bought his freedom and was officially ordained a minister. A few years later he built Georgia's first Black Baptist church in Savannah. After his death in 1812, Andrew

Bryan's tombstone was inscribed with these words: "He has done more among the poor slaves than all the learned doctors [scholars] in America. He was imprisoned for the Gospel [and] whipped, but was willing to suffer death for the cause of Christ. He was an honor to human nature, an ornament to religion, and a friend to mankind."[36]

> "He was an honor to human nature, an ornament to religion, and a friend to mankind."[36]
>
> —From the tombstone epitaph of early Black preacher Andrew Bryan

Black Churches

Jonathan and Andrew Bryan's preaching did more than Christianize Black slaves. It also put colonial and early US African Americans on the path to the cherished custom of worshipping in predominantly Black churches. And in turn, such specialized Christian worship helped shape the unique American Black identity that permeates the national African American community today. Indeed, the struggle for equal treatment that has been present throughout the Black American experience has been mirrored by the activities of the Black churches. This is because those institutions were, and still are, sustained and motivated by the concept of freedom.

The term *Black churches* refers mainly to Protestant denominations, including, among others, the National Baptist Convention, the African Methodist Episcopal Church, and the Church of God in Christ. According to a 2021 survey by the Pew Research Center, 66 to 67 percent of Black Americans are members of congregations affiliated with such groups. Of the remainder of African Americans, the study found, about 6 percent are Catholic; 3 percent belong to other Christian denominations, such as Jehovah's Witnesses; 3 percent are Muslims and other non-Christians; and roughly 21 percent are either nonreligious or choose not to belong to specific churches.

From the standpoint of standard Christian beliefs, including those surrounding Jesus and the Bible, Black ministers frequently

This 1941 photo shows Black women at a church in Woodville, Georgia. Throughout history, Black churches have been sustained and motivated by the concept of freedom.

deliver sermons relating to strictly religious topics. However, just as often they break tradition somewhat and talk frankly, and at times passionately, about current social and political issues, including the right to vote, racial equality, criminal justice reform, and others. Another way that Black churches often break tradition is through the free expression of emotions by the congregants. As the Pew Research Center survey pointed out, about 94 percent of the Black congregants interviewed described people impulsively calling out "amen" or other expressions of approval during services. In addition, it is not uncommon in these churches for worshippers to dance, jump, and/or shout spontaneously during a service.

Such outward emotional expression, along with discussions of freedom and justice, seen in the Black churches has contributed mightily to the modern African American identity. Noted documentary film producer Marilyn Mellowes summarizes this phenomenon, saying:

> For more than 300 years, the black church in America has provided a safe haven for Black Christians in a nation shadowed by the legacy of slavery and a society that remains defined by race and class. Inspired by the story of Exodus, African Americans can think out, pray out and shout out their anger and aspirations, free from the unstated yet powerful constraints that govern dialogue with the larger white society. In the pulpit and the pews, in choir lofts and Sunday schools, the Black church continues to offer affirmation and dignity to people still searching for equality and justice, still willing to reach out for a more inclusive, embracing tomorrow.[37]

Exploring Cultural Roots

Part of that search includes learning about one's origins. A great deal of personal history and identity were lost to slavery. For over two centuries Black slaves were denied the ability to connect with or celebrate their family history. Not only were those ties brutally severed by slave traders, once the slaves were in America, any newly formed family connections were often fleeting, as spouses, parents, children, and siblings were sold off to different owners. As a result, Black slaves had little or no chance of learning about, sharing, or celebrating their family heritage.

Later, however, in the mid-twentieth century, in the wake of that era's flurry of civil rights advances, the question of racial identity came to the fore for many Black Americans. Most knew that their ancestors had originated in Africa. But now they began asking specifically *where* in Africa and when and how those forebears

"The Black church continues to offer affirmation and dignity to people still searching for equality."[37]

—Documentary film producer Marilyn Mellowes

came to America. Hence, growing numbers of Black Americans started seeking out their family history and connections.

This explains the tremendous popularity of the 1977 ABC-TV miniseries *Roots*, based on the 1976 best-selling novel by African American writer Alex Haley. Drawing some 100 million viewers—still a television record—it depicted the enslavement of a young African, his journey to the America South, and his experiences there, as well as those of his immediate descendants. *Roots* was

The 1977 miniseries *Roots* was extremely popular. This still from the series shows actor LeVar Burton, as the protagonist Kunta Kinte/Toby.

Younger Blacks Know Less About Their Past

The history of Black slavery in America is well known. Not surprisingly, slavery and the Black struggle for freedom over the centuries have strongly shaped the Black American identity. However, the depth of knowledge about that aspect of African American history differs by age. This was one of the findings of the Pew Research Center's 2021 survey of Black Americans. The study found that 40 percent of Black adults under age thirty are unsure about whether their ancestors were actually slaves. Moreover, an even larger proportion of Blacks under age thirty—59 percent—told the Pew Research Center interviewers that they had rarely, if ever, spoken to their older family members about family history. Those same younger adults were also far less likely than their older relatives to have looked for information about their ancestors using one of the many online genealogy services.

an enormous hit, Dartmouth College scholar Matthew F. Delmont explains, because the "story asked readers and viewers across racial lines . . . to identify with the sorrow, pain, and joy of enslaved black families in ways that were . . . unprecedented on broadcast television. It [also reminded] African Americans, especially younger ones, about how their African roots partially shaped their identities."[38]

The same drive to understand Black family background and personal identity that inspired the production of *Roots* has continued to motivate subsequent generations of Black Americans. In recent years hundreds of thousands of them have turned to online search portals that help trace genealogical and other historical records. These searches can be invigorating but also frustrating. Records of ancestry for descendants of slaves are often either nonexistent or incomplete.

Even so, several organizations now regularly take Black Americans on excursions to African nations so they can connect with that piece of their identity. One such group, New York City–based Birthright Africa, provides free trips to Africa for young Black Americans who seek to explore their cultural roots. The participants visit cultural sites, museums, universities, and when possible actually meet local people to whom they may be distantly related. New York–born Shaina Louis, age twenty-three, took a Birthright Africa trip to Ghana in 2018. After hoping for years to find out where important aspects of her personal identity were rooted, she described the trip as a major eye-opener. She and the Africans with whom she shares ancestors "may not speak the same language," she told a CNN interviewer. "But the foods we eat, the way we carry ourselves, the way we relate to one another, and our deeply ingrained spirituality reflect a bond that is still there. There is a sense of inner peace and ease I now have, that wasn't there before. I can move forward with my life, with intention behind everything I do."[39]

Black Institutions of Higher Learning

For many young Black Americans, that process of moving forward has been aided by education at one of the nation's historically Black colleges and universities, also known as HBCUs. The first HBCU, Cheyney University (originally known as the African Institute), was established in 1837 in Pennsylvania. Dozens of others have opened since that time. Most were established between 1865 and 1900, during an era in which institutionalized bias and segregation prevented many Black young adults from obtaining higher education. Among the HBCUs established during this period were Howard University in Washington, DC; Alabama State University; Morehouse College in Georgia; and Morgan State University in Maryland. As of 2020 the National Center for Education Statistics listed 101 HBCUs in nineteen states, the District of Columbia, and the US Virgin Islands.

Thanks to such institutions, an increasing number of Black Americans have made their marks on society. They include scientists like George Washington Carver, educators like Booker T. Washington, novelists like James Weldon Johnson, historians like W.E.B. Du Bois, and doctors, lawyers, inventors, engineers, and many more.

In addition to helping shape American society overall, for many students the HBCUs have furthered the process of embracing identity. Standard university-level coursework is paired with courses that explore African history, music, arts, and oral traditions. But these courses are only one reason why many young Black Americans chose to attend the HBCUs. Long after US colleges and universities opened to all students regardless of race or ethnicity, the HBCUs remain a top choice for many.

Among Black college-bound students who recently made that choice is Maryland resident SeKai Parker. Accepted at sixteen different schools, among them Yale and other elite and predominantly White universities, she surprised many of her relatives when she announced she would be attending Spelman College, an HBCU in Atlanta. In a *New York Times* interview, Parker explained that she had concerns about possibly feeling isolated and unable to express herself completely among the mostly White students at

Most Black colleges and universities were established between 1865 and 1900, when institutionalized bias and segregation prevented many Black young adults from obtaining higher education. This picture shows the Howard University graduating class of 1900.

Yale. "College is the time when you're trying to figure out who you are," she said. "It's impossible to figure that out in a space where you not only feel like you have to assimilate to fit into that space, when they didn't invite you there or they tolerate you there, but you have to prove that your existence has value."[40]

> "College is the time when you're trying to figure out who you are. It's impossible to figure that out in a space where you not only feel like you have to assimilate to fit into that space, when they didn't invite you there or they tolerate you there, but you have to prove that your existence has value."[40]
>
> —College-bound Maryland teenager SeKai Parker

Pioneering Black Musicians

The Black American identity has also been influenced and shaped in part by music. Singing as a form of communication was common among enslaved Africans. Often during the torturous Atlantic crossings, slaves trapped in ships' cargo holds sang to one another to pass on information or express their pain and anger. As this music passed from one generation to another, it became an integral part of slave culture in America.

Thus, by the late nineteenth century, that culture possessed a unique musical heritage that eventually led to the creation of new, highly original styles. Notable among these were jazz and the blues. The roots of jazz, for instance, lay in New Orleans in the late 1800s. There Black musicians, many of whom could not read music, experimented with improvised, freestyle rhythms and melodies in music performed in small-scale local parades and family gatherings. This highly appealing sound soon moved into nightclubs. By 1917 an increasing number of White musicians began copying early Black Jazz and brought it into the American musical mainstream. It swiftly became so popular across the country and beyond that the 1920s came to be called the Jazz Age.

Several other popular musical styles also began in Black musical circles and were later "borrowed" by White musicians. They

Discrimination Based on Hairstyle

It is a sad fact that many of the elaborate and visually stunning hairstyles that originated in Africa and were adopted by Black American culture were often belittled by White society before the mid- to late twentieth century. Stereotyping of and discrimination against Black people based on their hairstyle was common (and still is in some quarters), as London fashion editor Kara Kia explains here.

> Many Black hairstyles have been historically labelled as "ghetto," "rough," "unprofessional," or otherwise used to dehumanize Black people. . . . The difference between Black women wearing blond and straight weaves and non-Black women wearing culturally Black hairstyles is that blond and straight hair does not have a painful history of discrimination that it's been trying to escape for at least the past 230 years. The discrimination against Black hairstyles has not only fueled the [pigeon-holing] of Black people but also the exclusion of Black communities from creating generational wealth and stability for their families. Stereotypes around Black hair . . . have literally kept Black women from work and education, making it more difficult to be financially independent members of society.

Kara Kia, "The Reason Non-Black People Should Not Wear Black Hairstyles Is Actually Very Simple," PopSugar, August 31, 2020. www.popsugar.com.

---

include ragtime, rock and roll, and in more recent times hip-hop and rap. In the words of university professors Portia K. Maultsby and Earl Stewart, Black musicians continue "to create new and distinctive styles of [music] in the tradition of African music-making that defined their unique African American identity."[41]

Indeed, music remains an important identity-shaping factor. It is one of a broad spectrum of cultural attributes and experiences that make Black Americans feel and identify as Black, including Black churches, Black colleges and universities, and Black celebrations of African origins. As California State University professor M. Keith Claybrook Jr. points out, for numerous Blacks that identity has become a sort of badge of pride. It is, he says, one way to bring "people of African descent human respect and dignity."[42]

CHAPTER FIVE

Facing Challenges

On July 16, 2016, a thirty-two-year-old Black man named Philando Castile was driving on a highway in St. Anthony, Minnesota, a suburb of Minneapolis. His girlfriend and her four-year-old daughter were also in the car. Unexpectedly, Castile saw the flashing lights of a police cruiser behind him and pulled over. The cruiser stopped nearby, and St. Anthony officer Jeronimo Yanez got out and walked to the open window of Castile's vehicle.

Like many Black men in America, as a youngster Castile had heard "the talk" from a parent. As his mother later explained, she had told him to be especially careful when it came to police and the justice system. Blacks, particularly Black males, she explained, tend to be suspected of crimes more often than Whites. Moreover, she added, it is extremely common for police to stop and question Black males in public. Always be polite during such a stop, she said, and never make any sudden movements. Otherwise, the officer might shoot first and ask questions later. Above all, she said, if Castile ever owned a gun, he should "always tell a police officer that he had a licensed firearm should he ever be pulled over."[43] That way, he could not be accused of secretly brandishing a weapon and thereby spooking the officer into drawing his own gun.

Castile remembered his mother's words when Yanez stopped him. A dashcam video shows that Castile remained calm and polite. And the first thing he did was tell Yanez, "Sir, I have to tell you I do have a firearm on me."[44] Although he did exactly what he had always been told to do, it was not enough. The video shows that Yanez became tense and agitated. And when Castile reached to get his license and registration, the officer curtly ordered him not to pull the gun out. Castile responded that he was *not* reaching for the gun, and his girlfriend politely told Yanez the same thing.

But it was too late. One or two seconds later, Yanez opened fire and quickly discharged seven shots. Five smashed through Castile's body. Despite the carnage, it seemed incredible to Castile's girlfriend, mother, friends, and much of the American public that a year later a jury acquitted Yanez of second-degree manslaughter. Its members apparently believed him when he told the court that he had fired his gun because he feared for his life.

> "Sir, I have to tell you I do have a firearm on me."[44]
>
> —Black driver Philando Castile to the police officer who stopped him

Blacks More Likely to Be Stopped or Killed

One question that many members of the media, as well as ordinary citizens, asked in the months that followed was *why* had the officer feared Castile so much? Another crucial question was whether Yanez would have been that afraid had Castile been White. Moreover, this was not the first time that people had asked such questions. That is because police shootings of Black people, especially Black men, have become common in the United States.

This was precisely why Castile's mother had given him "the talk." Perhaps more than most other members of society, Black parents are aware that large numbers of White people perceive most Black males to be dishonest, violent, dangerous, or all of those things. This unfair stereotyping and targeting of Black men and boys is one of the modern challenges that the American Black community faces on a regular basis.

The evidence that Blacks are frequently and unfairly targeted this way is substantial. First, numerous examples of such police violence aimed at Blacks have been, as in the Castile case, caught on camera. There is also ample statistical evidence. A 2020 study conducted by researchers at Stanford University and New York University found that out of about 100 million traffic stops across

Philando Castile was shot by a police officer in 2016. This photo shows a picture of Castile on the gate of the Minnesota governor's St. Paul residence, as protesters demonstrate against the shooting.

the United States, Black drivers were 20 percent more likely to be stopped than White drivers. Furthermore, the study showed, among all who were stopped, Blacks were searched almost twice as often as Whites, even though White drivers were actually *more* likely to be carrying guns, drugs, or other illegal items.

Moreover, an unexpectedly high percentage of Black Americans are killed each year by police. A forty-year study conducted by the world-renowned *Lancet* medical journal found that from 1980 to 2019, Black Americans were 3.5 times more likely to die at the hands of police than White Americans. Other studies have reported similarly disturbing findings. One conducted by the *Washington Post* from 2015 to 2021 found that although Blacks make up only 14 percent of the population, 24 percent of the roughly six thousand fatal shootings by police during those years were of African Americans.

A Long History of Discrimination

This sort of blatant bias is hardly new, says a team of researchers headed by Harvard University scholar Elizabeth Hinton. "Discriminatory criminal justice policies and practices," they report,

> have historically and unjustifiably targeted black people [in part] to continue post-slavery control over newly-freed people. This discrimination continues today in often less overt ways, including through disparity in the enforcement of seemingly race-neutral laws. For example, while rates of drug use are similar across racial and ethnic groups, Black people are arrested and sentenced on drug charges at much higher rates than White people.[45]

Indeed, the rates of incarceration for Blacks are out of proportion, considering the number of Blacks versus the number of Whites in society. Multiple studies indicate, for instance, that although Black men make up 13 percent of the male population, they constitute 35 percent of the overall US male prison population. Put another way, 1 in 3 Black males will spend at least some time in jail at one point or another, whereas only 1 in 17 White men will. (Similarly, 1 in 18 Black women serve at least some jail time, compared to 1 in 111 White women who do so.)

> "Black people are arrested and sentenced on drug charges at much higher rates than White people."[45]
>
> —Harvard University scholar Elizabeth Hinton

As studies show, this is *not* because Blacks commit more crimes than Whites. In addition to the fact that Whites use illegal drugs at the same rates that Blacks do, Hinton and her fellow researchers point out, "White Americans overestimate the share of burglaries, illegal drug sales, and juvenile crime committed by Black people by approximately 20 to 30 percent."[46]

Coming Together to Protest

These disparities have led to numerous calls for changes in policing, the justice system, and society in general to make the treatment of Black Americans fairer and more in line with the treatment of Whites. Some experts argue that new federal laws or serious attention to enforcing existing laws are needed. In an article for New York's Brennan Center for Justice, for example, Judge Taryn A. Merkl writes, "The federal government must renew [the] national commitment to civil rights"[47] that it embraced in the 1960s.

Other efforts to reform the system have come from ordinary citizens banning together to protest and demand change. Particularly prominent in this regard has been the work of Black Lives Matter (BLM). A loosely organized social movement consisting of citizens of all races, it opposes racial inequality and discrimination against Black people. BLM formed in 2013 to protest the acquittal of the man charged with the 2012 killing of a Black teenager, Trayvon Martin. The movement has grown larger and more influential over time, especially after George Floyd's murder in 2020. BLM protests have attracted many thousands of people in cities nationwide and in other countries.

Black Lives Matter protests have attracted thousands of people in cities nationwide and in other countries. This photo shows a BLM protest in June 2020, in Harrisburg, Pennsylvania.

Changes in Policing Methods

Chokeholds, once a common tactic used by police in subduing and arresting suspects, are now banned by many law enforcement agencies. This change resulted in large part from protests over the 2020 murder of George Floyd by a Minneapolis police officer. The officer knelt on Floyd's neck for over nine minutes, cutting off his air flow. During 2020 and 2021 police departments in twenty-three US cities banned chokeholds and other potentially dangerous holds and maneuvers. Among the cities making this change was Minneapolis, which banned chokeholds and other applications of physical trauma to the neck area.

The federal government has also made a similar change. In September 2021 the US Department of Justice prohibited federal officers from using chokeholds. In the memo that announced the change, Deputy Attorney General Lisa O. Monaco stated, "It is essential that law enforcement across the Department of Justice adhere to a single set of standards when it comes to 'chokeholds.'"

Quoted in US Department of Justice, "Department of Justice Announces Department-Wide Policy on Chokeholds and 'No-Knock' Entries," September 14, 2021. www.justice.gov.

Supporters of BLM point out that its protests, and those of other similar groups, have already brought about positive changes. One often cited example is the banning of police chokeholds, which had killed Black men during arrests in California, Texas, Nevada, and other states. Another reform inspired by citizen protests has been the adoption of body and dashboard cameras by numerous police departments. Few think that such changes will, by themselves, end discrimination against Black Americans. But such reforms are widely seen as important first steps in that direction.

Disparities in Education and Earnings

Educational disparities are an ongoing concern among Black Americans. For generations the proportion of Blacks who graduated from high school was significantly lower than the proportion of Whites. In recent years that situation has improved considerably. In 2021, according to the US Census Bureau, 90.3 percent of Black high school seniors graduated, a rate only slightly lower the 95.1 percent of White seniors who did so.

The disparity remains greater, however, when it comes to college education. The US Census Bureau reports that of Blacks age twenty-five years or older, roughly 28 percent have earned at least a bachelor's degree (four years of college). In comparison, about 42 percent of Whites age twenty-five or older have done so.

Experts say that poverty and lack of funding for many urban high schools with large Black populations contribute to the educational disparities between Black and White Americans. Another reason that fewer young Black men go to college is the fact that one in three of them spend at least some time in jail. And in the current system, people who have a felony on their records have extremely limited access to federal and other types of student loans. "To improve the economic outcomes for Black men," says Ashleigh Maciolek, formerly of Washington, DC's Brookings Institution, "there needs to be a policy response to these educational disparities. First, federal student loans should be made available to those with a felony conviction because it will provide many Black males with the opportunity to further their education."[48]

A diverse group of friends graduate from high school. In 2021, according to one study, 90.3 percent of Black high school seniors graduated, a rate only slightly lower than the 95.1 percent of White seniors who did so.

The Poverty Factor

In an article written for New York's Vera Institute of Justice, Harvard University scholar Elizabeth Hinton and her colleagues point out that negative attitudes about Black men by many White people stem partly from the problems of poverty, racism, and inequality. The rate of poverty, they explain, is much higher among Black people than among White people.

> The realities of poverty disproportionately affect Black people: 22 percent of Black people lived in poverty in 2016, compared to approximately 9 percent of White people. Thus, higher rates of poverty and the cumulative effects of structural racism mean Black people are exposed to the structural risk factors that make crime more likely at greater rates than their White counterparts. Compounded with justice system laws and practices that have disparate impacts and bias among [those accused of crimes], Black people are consequently arrested for certain crimes at higher rates. Put differently, racial disparities in the justice system are deeply rooted in historical racism that manifests today in structural inequalities—from the differences in the quality of education to unemployment rates to household wealth.

Elizabeth Hinton et al., "An Unjust Burden: The Disparate Treatment of Black Americans in the Criminal Justice System," Vera Institute of Justice, 2018. www.vera.org.

Education is often tied to earnings. But even when Black and White Americans have the same credentials and qualifications, Black Americans tend to earn less money. This trend was documented in a study conducted from 2017 to 2019 by PayScale, a company that analyzes job market data. The study concluded, "Even as black or African American men climb the corporate ladder, they still make less than equally qualified white men." More specifically, says PayScale's Jackson Gruver, the data show that the "pay gap for black men is $0.98 for every dollar a white man with the same qualifications makes. To put that in perspective, the median salary of a white man in our sample is $72,900; [in contrast, the] median pay for black or African American men is thus $71,500. This suggests a $1,400 difference in pay that is likely attributable to race."[49]

Replacing Outmoded Policies

Whether the challenge is to make sure Black people have equal opportunities in jobs and earnings, education, or interactions with police and the justice system, the burning question remains: when will American society allow full parity among all racial and ethnic groups, including African Americans? Among the many groups currently working to bring about these changes is the American Civil Liberties Union. Reaching true equality, its directors say, will not be easy, but they insist that it is achievable. The most realistic goal, they suggest, is to replace older, unfair policies with more up-to-date, fairer ones. Anti-Black racism, they continue,

> "Our history has shown us that it's not enough to take racist policies off the books if we are going to achieve true justice."[50]
>
> —A spokesperson for the American Civil Liberties Union

has played an active role in . . . virtually every [facet] of life since this nation's founding. Our history has shown us that it's not enough to take racist policies off the books if we are going to achieve true justice. Those past policies have structured our society and created deeply-rooted patterns and practices that can only be disrupted and reformed with new policies of similar strength and efficacy. . . . The goal is to build a nation where every person can achieve their highest potential.[50]

SOURCE NOTES

Introduction: The Diversity of Black Americans

1. Kiana Cox and Christine Tamir, "Race Is Central to Identity for Black Americans and Affects How They Connect with Each Other," Pew Research Center, April 14, 2022. www.pewresearch.org.
2. Alex Wade, "African Americans: We Are Not Monolithic," First 5 Los Angeles, February 10, 2022. www.first5la.org.
3. Quoted in Jennifer Agiesta and Ariel Edwards-Levy, "Pew Poll: Being Black Is Central to Sense of Identity for Most Black Americans," CNN, April 14, 2022. www.cnn.com.
4. Quoted in Maquita Peters, "Being Black in America: We Have a Place in This World Too," NPR, June 5, 2020. www.npr.org.
5. Quoted in Peters, "Being Black in America."
6. Kiana Cox and Christine Tamir, "Race Is Central to Identity for Black Americans."

Chapter One: Coming to America

7. Quoted in *Africans in America*, "Equiano's Autobiography," PBS. www.pbs.org.
8. Quoted in *Africans in America*, "Equiano's Autobiography."
9. Irwin Unger, *These United States: The Questions of Our Past, vol. 1, To 1877*. Upper Saddle River, NJ: Prentice Hall, 2007, p. 288.
10. Quoted in National Humanities Center, "Runaway Slave Advertisements, 1745–1775: A Selection." https://nationalhumanitiescenter.org.
11. Unger, *These United States*, p. 288.
12. Henry Louis Gates Jr., "Free Blacks Lived in the North, Right?," PBS, 2013. www.pbs.org.
13. Quoted in David Lodge, "John Randolph's Slaves," Shelby County Historical Society, 1998. www.shelbycountyhistory.org.
14. Quoted in Lauren A. Floyd, "Conversations on Race and Identity with Black Immigrants," USC StorySpace, 2017. https://uscstoryspace.com.
15. Quoted in Floyd, "Conversations on Race and Identity with Black Immigrants."
16. Quoted in Floyd, "Conversations on Race and Identity with Black Immigrants."

Chapter Two: Striving for Rights

17. William Wells Brown, *Narrative of William W. Brown, a Fugitive Slave, Written by Himself*. Project Gutenberg, 2005. www.gutenberg.org.
18. Quoted in Bill of Rights Institute, "Frederick Douglass, Narrative of the Life of Frederick Douglass, 1845," 2022. https://billofrightsinstitute.org.
19. Quoted in Milton Meltzer, ed., *The Black Americans: Their History in Their Own Words, 1619–1983*. New York: Crowell, 1984, pp. 65–66.

20. Equal Justice Initiative, "Lynching in America: Confronting the Legacy of Racial Terror," 2022. https://eji.org.
21. Quoted in Nikole Hannah-Jones, ed., *The 1619 Project*. New York: One World, 2021, p. 272.
22. Quoted in Libby Neidenbach, "Homer Plessy and the Black Activists Who Fought Segregation All the Way to the Supreme Court," Historic New Orleans Collection, March 4, 2021. www.hnoc.org.
23. Quoted in History.com, "'I Have a Dream' Speech," January 7, 2022. www.history.com.
24. Quoted in Library of Congress, "The Civil Rights Era: Sit-Ins, Freedom Rides, and Demonstrations." https://memory.loc.gov.

Chapter Three: Building Community

25. James Truslow Adams, *Epic of America*. New York: Blue Ribbon, 1931, p. 404.
26. Quoted in Arpita Aneja and Olivia B. Waxman, "Beyond Tulsa: The Historic Legacies and Overlooked Stories of America's 'Black Wall Streets,'" *Time*, May 28, 2021. https://time.com.
27. Quoted in National Park Service, "The St. Luke's Penny Savings Bank," February 9, 2022. www.nps.gov.
28. Brianna Rhodes, "9 Historic Black Neighborhoods That Celebrate Black Excellence," National Trust for Historic Preservation, October 15, 2020. https://savingplaces.org.
29. Paul Gardullo, "The Roots of Greenwood," National Museum of African American History and Culture. https://nmaahc.si.edu.
30. Amber Gibson, "The Rise, Fall, and Rise Again of 'Black Wall Street,'" Greenwood Rising. www.greenwoodrising.org.
31. Quoted in Gibson, "The Rise, Fall, and Rise Again of 'Black Wall Street.'"
32. Dee Dee Green, "Building Sustainable and Equitable Black Communities," American Friends Service Committee, April 28, 2021. www.afsc.org.
33. Quoted in Green, "Building Sustainable and Equitable Black Communities."
34. Quoted in Ben Adlin, "Africatown Speaker Series Explores How to Build Thriving Black Communities," South Seattle Emerald, July 5, 2022. https://southseattleemerald.com.
35. Rhodes, "9 Historic Black Neighborhoods That Celebrate Black Excellence."

Chapter Four: Embracing Identity

36. Quoted in J.H. Redding, *Life and Times of Jonathan Bryan, 1708–1788*. Savanah, GA: Morning News Print, 1901, p. 44.
37. Marilyn Mellowes, "The Black Church," PBS. www.pbs.org.
38. Matthew F. Delmont, "Why America Forgot About *Roots*," *New York Times*, May 27, 2016. www.nytimes.com.

39. Quoted in Alaa Elasser, "Young Black Americans Who Want to Explore Their Roots Can Take a Free Birthright Trip to Africa. Here's How," CNN, February 3, 2020. www.cnn.com.
40. Quoted in Erica L. Green, "Why Students Are Choosing H.B.C.U.s: '4 Years Being Seen as Family,'" *New York Times*, June 11, 2022. www.nytimes.com.
41. Portia K. Maultsby and Earl Stewart, "African Origins and Adaptations in African American Music," Timeline of African American Music, 2021. https://timeline.carnegiehall.org.
42. M. Keith Claybrook Jr., "Black Identity and the Power of Self-Naming," African American Intellectual History Society, September 10, 2021. www.aaihs.org.

Chapter Five: Facing Challenges

43. Quoted in Melissa Noel, "'You Could Be Next': Philando Castile's Mom Speaks Out on Police Brutality," NBC News, August 27, 2017. www.nbcnews.com.
44. Quoted in Jay Croft, "Philando Castile Shooting: Dashcam Video Shows Rapid Event," CNN, June 21, 2017.
45. Elizabeth Hinton et al., "An Unjust Burden: The Disparate Treatment of Black Americans in the Criminal Justice System," Vera Institute of Justice, 2018. www.vera.org.
46. Hinton et al., "An Unjust Burden."
47. Taryn A, Merkl, "Protecting Against Police Brutality and Official Misconduct," Brennan Center for Justice, April 29, 2021. www.brennancenter.org.
48. Ashleigh Maciolek, "6 Policies to Address Social Problems Affecting Black Boys and Men," Brookings Institution, 2020. www.brookings.edu.
49. Jackson Gruver, "Racial Age Gap for Men," PayScale, May 7, 2019. www.payscale.com.
50. ReNika Moore and Rakim Brooks, "To End Systematic Racism, Ensure Systematic Equality," American Civil Liberties Union, February 8, 2021. www.aclu.org.

FOR FURTHER RESEARCH

Books

Alverne Ball and Stacey Robinson, *Across the Tracks: Remembering Greenwood, Black Wall Street, and the Tulsa Race Massacre*. New York: Abrams ComicArts Megascope, 2021.

Stephen Currie, *Important Black Americans in Civil Rights and Politics*. San Diego: ReferencePoint, 2022.

Don Nardo, *Important Black Americans in Science and Invention*. San Diego: ReferencePoint, 2022.

Lanze Thompson, *Black Wounds: The Pains, Scars, and Triumphs of Black America*. Independently published, 2021.

Margeaux Weston, *20th Century Black American History for Kids*. New York: Rockridge, 2021.

Internet Sources

Bullock Museum, "Buffalo Soldiers." www.thestoryoftexas.com.

Eric Herschthal, "Black Americans Have Always Understood Science as a Tool in Their Freedom Struggle," May 18, 2021. www.washingtonpost.com.

IFT Foundation, "8 Black Scientific Pioneers Who Forever Changed Food." www.ift.org.

Live Science Staff, "Amazing Black Scientists," Live Science, June 10, 2020. www.livescience.com.

Christina Pazzanese, "How Unjust Police Killings Damage the Mental Health of Black Americans," *Harvard Gazette*, May 13, 2021. https://news.harvard.edu.

David Remnick, "Hollywood's Fraught History with Black Audiences," *New Yorker*, February 28, 2022. www.newyorker.com.

Brianna Rhodes, "9 Historic Black Neighborhoods That Celebrate Black Excellence," National Trust for Historic Preservation, October 15, 2020. https://savingplaces.org.

Amy D. Sorkin, "Judge Ketanji Brown Jackson's Historic Nomination to the Supreme Court," *New Yorker*, February 25, 2022. www.newyorker.com.

Christine Tamir, "The Growing Diversity of Black America," Pew Research Center, March 15, 2021. www.pewresearch.org.

Websites
African American Heritage, National Archives
www.archives.gov/research/african-americans
This enormous website has links to hundreds of articles and blogs about African American history and culture, as well as individual people, events, legal battles, and much more.

African American Perspectives, Library of Congress
www.loc.gov/collections/african-american-perspectives-rare-books/about-this-collection
Documents on this site present an expansive view of African American history and culture, primarily from the years between 1822 and 1909. This includes original works of influential Black Americans and other materials that can be accessed through the "Collection Items" and "Articles and Essays" links.

African Americans in World War II, National World War II Museum
www.nationalww2museum.org/war/topics/african-americans-world-war-ii
This enlightening and useful site, presented by the national World War II Museum, in New Orleans, contains oral histories, photographs, profiles of soldiers and sailors, and various objects that call attention to and honor African Americans who were part of the US World War II effort.

Black History Continued
www.nytimes.com
This series from the *New York Times* explores important events and influential people in Black history and culture. Articles explore a wide variety of topics including HBCUs, Black women in politics, Black outdoors pioneers, the Tulsa Race Massacre, Black hairstyles, Black comic superheroes, and much more.

George Washington Carver National Monument, National Park Service History Library
http://npshistory.com/publications/gwca
The website for this national monument dedicated to George Washington Carver provides a short summary of his accomplishments, information about the monument itself, including what to look for in the woods surrounding the visitors' center. The website also includes links to numerous key documents relating to Carver and his inventions and achievements.

National Museum of African American History and Culture
https://nmaahc.si.edu
This is the newest of the Smithsonian Institution museums in Washington, DC. Users who click on "Explore" will find a wealth of information and historic photos by searching the collection and exploring exhibitions, stories, and initiatives.

INDEX

Note: Boldface page numbers indicate illustrations.

abolitionists and abolition
  Cary, 20
  escaped slaves
    Brown, 18, **19**
    Douglass, 19–20
    Equiano, 9–10, 14
    Garnet, 20
    Tubman, 20, **21**
  Garrison, 19
  goal of, 18
  in Maryland, 19
  slave trade abolished in Britain and US, 19
  Walker, 20–21
Adichie, Chimamanda Ngozi, 15–16
Africatown Community Land Trust (ACLT), 34–35
Africatown Plaza (Seattle, WA), 34–35
age and knowledge of ancestors as slaves, 41
age distribution, 4
Alabama State University, 42
Allen, Lecester, 31
Amadu, Nabil, 16, 17
American Civil Liberties Union, 54
"the American dream," 27
American Friends Service Committee (AFSC), 33–34
Appeal to the Coloured Citizens of the World (Walker), 20–21
armed forces
  Blacks in, during Civil War, 22
  Blacks in, during World War II, 24
  integration of, 24
Armstrong, Louis, 28
arts, Harlem Renaissance, 28

Baker, Josephine, 28
banking, 29
Birmingham, Alabama, 30
Birthright Africa, 41–42
Black Lives Matter (BLM), **50**, 50–51
Black Wall Street, 30–33, **32**
Boynton v. Virginia (1960), 25
Brennan Center for Justice, 50
Brown, Wells, 18
Brown, William Wells, 18
Brown v. Board of Education (1954), 24
Bryan, Andrew, 36–37
Bryan, Jonathan, 36
businesspeople
  Allen, 31
  Greenwood sector, 30–33, **32**
  Walker, 28–29, **29**

Carver, George Washington, 42
Cary, Mary Ann Shadd, 20
Castile, Philando, 46–47, **48**
Cheyney University, 42
chokeholds, police use of, 51
Christianity, Black churches, 36–39, **38**
civil rights
  Black churches and, 38, 39
  Civil Rights Act (1964) and, 26
  Freedom Riders, 25
  integration and, 24, 25
  laws challenged in courts, 23–24
  march in Washington, DC (2013), **16**
  March on Washington (1963), 25–26, **26**
  New Orleans Black social club, 23
  protests against racism in law enforcement, 8, **50**, 50–51
  Voting Rights Act (1965) and, 26
Civil Rights Act (1964), 26
Civil War (1861–1865), 21, 22
Claybrook, M. Keith, Jr., 45
communities
  Africatown Plaza (Seattle, Washington), 34–35

Black enclaves as safe spaces,
　　27–28
　Fourth Avenue District (Birmingham,
　　AL), 30
　Greenwood sector (Tulsa,
　　Oklahoma), 30–33, **32**
　Harlem (New York City), 28
　Jackson Ward in Richmond, Virginia,
　　28–30, **29**
　of third wave immigrants (1980–
　　2019), 15
Constitution, 21
Cooper, Venita, 33
countries of origin, 15, 16
Cox, Kiana, 6, 7
Crusader (newspaper), 23

Delmont, Matthew F., 41
discrimination. *See* racism
Douglass, Frederick, 19–20
drug arrests and sentences, 49
Du Bois, W.E.B., 42

education
　degrees attained, 4, 52
　funding of high schools with large
　　Black populations, 52
　high school graduation rate, 51, **52**
　historically Black colleges and
　　universities, 42–44, **43**
　income and, 53
　lack of books about Black immigrant
　　experience, 17
　poverty and, 52
　segregation of, 23, 24
　student loans and felony convictions,
　　52
Ellington, Duke, 28
Ellington, Jason, 8
entrepreneurs
　Allen, 31
　Greenwood sector, 30–33, **32**
　Walker, 28–29, **29**
equality, achieving true, 54
Equal Justice Initiative (EJI), 22
Equiano, Olaudah, 9–10, 14

Falconbridge, Alexander, 14

families during slavery, 12–13
Fifty-Fourth Massachusetts Regiment
　(Civil War), 22
Floyd, George, 8, 50, 51
food, New Orleans project, 34
Fourteenth Amendment (Constitution),
　21
Fourth Avenue District (Birmingham,
　AL), 30
Freedom Riders, 25

Gardullo, Paul, 31
Garnet, Henry H., 20
Garrett, K.W., 34–35, **35**
Garrett-Scott, Shennette, 27–28
Garrison, William Lloyd, 19
Garvey, Marcus, 28
Gates, Henry Louis, Jr., 13
Gibson, Amber, 32
Glory (film), 22
Green, Dee Dee, 33–34
Greensboro, North Carolina, 25
Greenwood Rising (museum), 33
Greenwood sector of Tulsa (OK),
　30–33, **32**
Gruver, Jackson, 53

hairstyles, 45
Haley, Alex, 40
Harlem (New York City), 28
"Harlem of the South" (Jackson Ward in
　Richmond, Virginia), 28–30, **29**
Harlem Renaissance, 28
Hinton, Elizabeth, 49, 53
historically Black colleges and
　universities (HBCUs), 42–44, **43**
Historic New Orleans Collection, 23
Howard University, 42, **43**
Hughes, Langston, 28
Hurston, Zora Neale, 28

identity
　Black churches and, 37, 38–39
　countries of origin and, 15–16
　importance of being Black to, 7
　music and, 44–45
　search for family history, 39–42, **40**
　slavery and, 41–42

"I Have a Dream" (King), 25–26, **26**
immigrants, 15
incarceration, 49, 52
income, 5, 53

Jackson Ward district (Richmond, Virginia), 28–30, **29**
jazz, 44
Jim Crow laws, 22
Johnson, James Weldon, 42
Johnson, Lyndon, 26

Kia, Kara, 45
King, Martin Luther, Jr., 25–26, **26**
Ku Klux Klan, 31

Lancet (journal), 48
law enforcement
  racism in
    basis of, 53
    drug arrests and sentences, 49
    incarceration rate, 49, 52
    police killings, 8, 46–47, 48, **48**, 50, 51
    protests against, 8, **50**, 50–51
    traffic stops and searches, 47–48
  "the talk" and, 46, 47
  use of chokeholds, 51
Lewis, John, 25
life expectancy, 4
Louis, Shaina, 42
lynchings, 22

Maciolek, Ashleigh, 52
March on Washington (1963), 25–26, **26**
Martin, Trayvon, 50
Maryland, 19
Maultsby, Portia K., 45
Mellowes, Marilyn, 39
Merkl, Taryn A., 50
Middle Passage, 9, **11**, 14
Minneapolis, 8, 51
Monaco, Lisa O., 51
Morehouse College, 42
Morgan State University, 42
music, 44–45

National Center for Education Statistics, 42
New Black Wall Street Market (Stonecrest, Georgia), 31
New Orleans, 23, 33–34
New York City, 28
New York Times (newspaper), 43–44
New York University, 47–48
North Star (newspaper), 20

occupations of third wave immigrants (1980—2019), 15
Ogundana, Ewaoluwa "Ewa," 17

Parker, SeKai, 43–44
Pascal, Michael Henry, 9
pay gap, 53
PayScale, 53
Penrice, Ronda Racha, 31
Pew Research Center
  basic facts about, 6
  Black congregants' expressions of approval during church services, 38
  Black knowledge of ancestors as slaves, 41
  on connection felt among diverse Black Americans, 8
  on importance of being Black to identity, 7
Pittman, Alexander, 8
Plessy, Homer, 24
Plessy v. Ferguson (1896), 24
population
  in 1860, 14
  current, 4
  diversity of, 6, **7**, 8
  of free Blacks in 1850s, 13
  states with largest Black, **5**
poverty, 53
prejudice. *See* racism
public accommodations, segregation of, 23–24, 25, 26

race, importance of, to identity, 7, **7**
racism
  destruction of Greenwood sector of Tulsa, Oklahoma, 30–33, **32**

62

hairstyles and, 45
in law enforcement
  basis of, 53
  drug arrests and sentences, 49
  incarceration rate, 49, 52
  police killings, 8, 46–47, 48, **48**, 50, 51
  protests against, 8, **50**, 50–51
  traffic stops and searches, 47–48
structural, and crime, 53
Randolph, John, 13–14
religion
  affiliations, **5**, 37
  Black churches, 36–39, **38**
  slaves and, 36
Rhodes, Brianna, 30, 35
Richmond, Virginia, 28–30, **29**
Robeson, Paul, 28
Rock Hill, South Carolina, 25
Roots (television miniseries), **40**, 40–41

segregation
  Civil Rights Act (1964) and, 26
  of education, 24
  Jim Crow laws, 22
  of transportation/public places, 23–24, 25
Shaw, Robert Gould, 22
slaves
  Black knowledge of ancestors as, 41–42
  Christianity and, 36
  Civil War and, 21
  escaped
    Brown, 18, **19**
    Douglass, 19–20
    Equiano, 9–10, 14
    Garnet, 20
    Tubman, 20, **21**
  family life of, 12–13
  freed by owners, 13–14
  infant mortality of, 11
  lives of, as property, 10–12, **13**
  music and, 44
  names of, 36
  trade in, 14
    abolished in Britain and US, 19

basic facts about, 10
Middle Passage, 9, **11**, 14
See also abolitionists and abolition
Spelman College, 43
St. Anthony, Minnesota, 46–47, **48**
St. Luke Herald (newspaper), 28
St. Luke Penny Savings, 29
Stanford University, 47–48
Stewart, Earl, 45
Stonecrest, Georgia, 31
Stradford Hotel, 30

"the talk," 46, 47
third wave immigrants (1980–2019), 15
Thirteenth Amendment (Constitution), 21
transportation, segregation of
  Civil Rights Act (1964) and, 26
  Freedom Riders and, 25
  Supreme Court decisions about, 23–24
Truman, Harry, 24
Tubman, Harriet, 20, **21**

Underground Railroad, 20
Unger, Irwin, 10, 12
US Census Bureau, 51, 52
US Supreme Court, segregation decisions by, 24, 25
U-Street in Washington, DC, 30

Vera Institute of Justice, 53
voting, 22
Voting Rights Act (1965), 26

Wade, Alex, 6
wage gap, 53
Walker, David, 20–21
Walker, Maggie L., 28–29, **29**
Washington, Booker T., 42
Washington, DC, **16**, 30
Washington Post (newspaper), 48
Wells, Ida B., 23
"We Shall Overcome," 26
World War II, 24

Yanez, Jeronimo, 46–47

PICTURE CREDITS

Cover: Shutterstock.com

4: Top: aelitta/iStock (top right),
4: Maury Aaseng (chart)
4: Mega Pixel/Shutterstock (middle)
4: Monkey Business Images/Shutterstock
5: Maury Aaseng: map and pie chart
5: IYIKON/Shutterstock: (middle)
7: Monkey Business Images/Shutterstock
11: Peter Newark American Pictures/Bridgeman Images
13: Niday Picture Library/Alamy Stock Photo
16: Joseph Sohm/Shutterstock
20: Alpha Historical/Alamy Stock Photo
26: Associated Press
29: Randy Duchaine/Alamy Stock Photo
32: Science History Images/Alamy Stock Photo
35: Reuters/Alamy Stock Photo
38: Glasshouse Images/Alamy Stock Photo
40: Pictorial Press Ltd/Alamy Stock Photo
43: History and Art Collection/Alamy Stock Photo
48: Associated Press
50: Jeani Photography/Shutterstock
52: Ground Picture: Shuterstock.com

Sources: Black Americans by the Numbers
- Nicholas Jones, et al., "2020 Census Illuminates Racial and Ethnic Composition of the Country," US Census Bureau, August 12, 2021. www.census.gov.
- Christine Tamir, "The Growing Diversity of Black America," Pew Research Center, March 25, 2021. www.pewresearch.org.
- US Census Bureau, "Census Bureau Releases New Educational Attainment Data," February 24, 2022. www.census.gov.
- "Profile: Black/African Americans," U.S. Department of Health and Human Services Office of Minority Health, October 12, 2021. https://minorityhealth.hhs.gov.
- Christine Tamir, "The Growing Diversity of Black America," Pew Research Center, March 25, 2021. www.pewresearch.org.
- Besheer Mohamed, et al, "Faith Among Black Americans," Pew Research Center, February 16, 2021. www.pewresearch.org.